B Metchim

Wild West Poems

B Metchim

Wild West Poems

ISBN/EAN: 9783744661843

Printed in Europe, USA, Canada, Australia, Japan

Cover: Foto ©Thomas Meinert / pixelio.de

More available books at **www.hansebooks.com**

Wild West Poems.

Composed and Illustrated

by

B. Metchim.

Second Edition.

London:
1892.

INDEX.

	PAGE
Concerning that B'ar and Tom Sullivan ...	1
An Unmentionable Injun...	6
A Snake Story—and don't you forget it ! ...	8
Song of Rainwather	11
A Slight Muddle	12
Buck Watkins	14
Died in his Boots	24
A Wail from Old Yurrup	26
Nature	28
Humanum Est	32
Gone Under...	33
D. Boone	34
Night	37
A Great Time	39
Sam Blackburn's Ride	43
Painting the Town Red	53
The Ghost Dance of the Indian Nations ...	58
At the Goal...	63
Let Sleeping Dogs Lie	65
"Like as a Father pitieth his Children" ...	67
Fancy	70
The Ocean	73
When Day is done	75
The Gentle Bronco	77
The Poet	78

		PAGE
Bonnie Dundee	... ...	79
The Indian Village	... ...	80
Alas! Poor Bertie	... ...	82
The Warning	... ...	83
"Lone Wolf," Died 1892	... ...	86
The Railway Men	... ...	88
Companions in Sin	... ...	90
Arms and a Hero	... ...	92
Fairyland	... ...	94
The Western States of America	... ...	95
Romancia in Absurdā	... ...	97

LIST OF ILLUSTRATIONS.

———

PAGE

FRONTISPIECE.

WHEN THE DARKNESS OF THE NIGHT IS OVER ... 28

THROUGH THE LEAFY BOUGHS 38

BUT BEWARE HOW THOU MAKEST THY FUTURE VOWS 52

GO FORTH! RETAKE YOUR NATIVE LAND 60

IN YOUR LAND SHALL BE MOURNING 85

THOSE LIQUID DEPTHS 94

Wild West Poems.

CONCERNING THAT B'AR AND TOM SULLIVAN.

HERE lived a chap in Texas once,
  Named Thomas Sullivan,
   Folks calculate thet Tommy was
  The head boss ugly man.

This luckless coon he was a boy
  With such an ugly face,
Thet anyone he met at night
  Would quicken up his pace.

Now Tom was great on grizzly b'ars,
  He'd yank up mighty yarns
About them thet would make you stare,
  They were so full of "darns."

But one he told to us surpassed
  In horror all the rest;
It was by far the tallest one
  With which we have been blest.

'Twas this:—Thet how one day he rode
  Upon his noble hoss,
Feeling thet he of all the whole
  Creation was the boss.

When on a suddent he espied
  The mightiest grizzly b'ar
He'd ever set his peepers on,
  And up went every hair.

The b'ar saw Tommy too, yew bet ;
  Tom lit down off his hoss ;
He made tracks slick, yew bet your boots,
  And hid among the moss.

The Coroner's inquest,—thet's the b'ar,—
  Fust sot upon the hoss,
And chawed him up, and then he went
  Fur Tom, the second course.

Thet child was squatted 'side a stump,
  He'd said his prayers thrice ;
He'd betted all his pile thet he'd
  Be gobbled in a trice.

But, fust, yew bet, he thought thet he
  Would quarrel fur his life,
So when he found he'd dropped his gun,
  He grabbed his bowie knife.

They hed a 20-furlong race,
  And Tommy didn't win ;
The b'ar rolled after him, just like
  A waggon load of sin.

The b'ar knocked Tommy down and made
  Him flatter than a bun ;
He kicked his bowie out of sight,
  And then began the fun.

His seven-shooter Tom had dropped
  Right at the fust set out ;
So he made up his mind tew hev
  A fisticuffing bout.

Tom stuck his spurs into the b'ar ;
  Old Ephraim only smiled ;
But he bit Tommy fur his cheek,
  Which made thet nigger wild.

Tom cussed and swore with all his strength,
  But did'nt quit the fight.
The b'ar he gathered Tommy in,
  And hugged with all his might.

He grabbed fur Tommy's beaky nose
  And sucked it in like jam,
Which made thet nigger use bad words,
  Some of which rhymed with Sam.

His rifle Tommy couldn't get
  'Twas just a bit too far ;
Besides, yew see, it wasn't the
  Intention of thet b'ar

Tew let young Tommy go just yet
   —The old iniquity—
But clawed thet coon right down his phiz
   Which spiled it, don't yer see.

They fit right smart from Saturday
   Intew the other week,
And then I calculate they got
   Tired of each other's cheek.

When thet b'ar found thet he could not
   Shorten the nigger's life,
He got real mad, and then they had
   The awfullest sorter strife.

He thought, at any rate, he'd spile
   The beauty of the coon,
And so he set about the work
   And did it mighty soon.

When Tommy found the darned b'ar hed
   Succeeded in his trick,
Namely, to spile his loveliness,
   He swore like Ancient Nick;

And rammed and jammed, and hit and kicked,
   'Twas all of no avail,
The b'ar would neither go himself
   Nor yet let Tom set sail.

At length he managed to escape,
  And, like greased lightning, sped
To where his faithful rifle lay,
  And filled it up with lead.

Tom says the rifle was so glad
  Tew see his master kum,
It ran tew meet him; but, yew bet,
  We don't believe thet hum.

Before thet b'ar could think a thought
  He'as shooted intew fits,
And Tom had nought tew back his tale
  But sundry little bits.

He'as so exhausted thet he slept
  Fur tew whole nights and days,
And when he woke he thought thet he
  Had better mend his ways.

But first he sot down and felt bad
  About thet grizzly b'ar;
He'd shot him intew kingdom kum
  And had not left a hair.

So when he tells the tale tew folks,
  They kinder sorter wink;
But he don't keer, he knows it's true.
  —Now kum and hev a drink.

AN UNMENTIONABLE INJUN.

I N Mexico, you all must know,
  An Injun lived, whose name
  Had twenty times as many rhymes
As men of far more fame.

'Twas Wha-cha-chin Je-whil-li-kin-
 Tony-ton-wo-whe-which,
And all this waste, in English placed,
 Means He-who-makes-you-twitch.

Well, one fine day in balmy May,
 This Injun got so tight,
He sprawled around upon the ground
 And swore that black was white.

He thought that he was Nancy Lee,
 Or some such personage ;
He got real mad, because he had
 To himself all the stage.

Four friends of his, around on biz,
 —A most unusual thing,
Drank all his grog and scragged his prog,
 And then began to sing.

They thought no sin to just step in
   And help themselves a heap ;
Then lay around upon the ground
   And all went off to sleep.

When Wha-cha-chin Je-whil-li-kin
   Rose two days later on,
He found his wife and scalping knife,
   Brandy and friends all gone.

He gave a yell and out pell mell
   He bolted there and then ;
He run a-muck and killed a duck,
   Four women and three men.

He ran so fast that just at last
   When things began to hum,
He rushed pell mell right into—Hongkong,
   Which frightened people some.

The boys all say that from that day
   That settlement out thar
Has nearly been quite free from sin ;
   A thing peculiar.

A SNAKE STORY—AND DON'T YOU
FORGET IT!

UM, squat around boys, while I spin
   A strictly truthful yarn,
   I won't use any naughty words
Like "cuss yer eyes" or "darn."

But spread myself considerable,
   Although 'twill hurt me sum,
And let yer hev the hull affair
   With nary bit of hum.

'Twas this-a-way: one day, I guess,
   I took it in my head
I'd foot it to the nearest store
   And paint the diggings red.

And so I took my shootin' irons,
   A tomahawk and knife,
Yew bet yer bottom dollar I
   Was fixed up for the strife.

I guess, I started right away
   When, just before my eyes!
I saw a snake upon a log,
   Of such a monstrous size,

I calculated thet thar was
   No earthly place like hum,
So I made tracks accordingly
   Fur I was frightened sum.

I reached the place and bolted in,
  The snake came in as well,
I made tall tracks and through the back
  I went, yew bet, pell mell.

The critter followed, like the tail
  Of much-abused Nick;
Yew can't imagine, strangers,
  How I hankered fur a stick

Tew help myself tew fly along,
  Fur I was getting done,
And badly used-up by thet most
  One-sided bit of fun.

I sailed across the prairie
  Like lightning on a spree;
Like an electric sausage it
  Came humping after me.

I cussed and prayed by turns, but thet's
  A mixture thet don't pay;
It does no good, and in my case
  'Tis best tew only pray.

At last I thought thet I should die
  If thet beast wouldn't quit;
My shirt had long deserted me,
  My breeches they were split.

My boots began tew think 'twas time
  Tew go about their biz;
The ground, tew, got most rough and vile,
  In humps and hills it riz.

About the middle of the day
  I calculated I
Hed had enough of thet 'ere game,
  An' fixed tew fight or die.

I faced around, and, gentlemen,
  I hope yew'll all sit still,
An' when I'm done we'll hev some grog,
  And each boy hev his fill.

I faced about, as I hev said,
  And—No, I wasn't chawed,
Although I's battered, bruised, and hurt,
  And very badly clawed.

If yew'll believe me, gentlemen,
  There'as nary thing in sight,
Except a little tree or tew,
  Ter give me any fright.

Yew needn't smile and wink like thet
  Unless yew want ter fight,
I say, as I'm a gentleman,
  I really wasn't tight.

SONG OF RAINWATHER.

ITTER patter, pitter patter,
    Fell the rain in merry England,
    Making all the people wish that
It would emigrate to Hades.
Raining, raining, ever raining,
Never ending, *toujours* raining,
Rushing, flooding, still descending
In one long and dreary current,
Raining on and raining ever.

Through the month of January
Down and down the rain it poureth;
March and February ditto,
April, May and June all ditto,
All the other months are ditto.
Raining, raining, raining, raining,
Always, ever, *toujours* raining,
All night long throughout it raineth,
In the morning, in the evening,
In the afternoon it raineth,
Raineth, raineth, raineth, raineth.

A SLIGHT MUDDLE.

–TRAVELLING once in Mexico
    Upon the Yankee stage,
      Were several boys, and women too,
  Of every size and age.

Old Dock, the driver, was a boy
  With a considerable
Amount of hatchet-throwing yarns,
  And 'twas a miracle

Of which old Dock was mighty proud,
  If any of them came
Within a mile or two of truth;
  But he was not to blame.

For seated, as he always was,
  Among a pack of boys
Whose yarns would raise yer scalp a heap,
  Which constitute their joys,

If he'd a kept from talking tall,
  Which he by no means had,
He'd probably have been laid out,
  The which would have been sad.

For if he'd been, nevertheless,
   I mean, considerably,
Oh cuss it, no! I don't mean that,
   I guess I'm getting mixed.

I'll start again : I mean if he
   Hed been laid out, you twig,
Thet things would—look'ee heer my boys
   I guess I'll take a swig.

I mean that if, or rather when,
   Or perhaps we'll say if how—
I guess if you start grinnin' thar
   We sail intew a row.

If he hed been, or when he'd been,
   Nevertheless, when, which,
How, what, if, thet, why, where the deuce,
   —Well this is gettin' rich.

I really can't express myself
   A bit more clear, I swear,
I rayther guess thet drink of yours
   Hes got among my hair.

BUCK WATKINS.

UT the Consul's brow was sad,
　　And the Consul's speech was low, (*very* low),
　　As he sot within the Senate house
And squinted at the foe.
"The Yanks will be upon us
　Before the bridge goes down;
And if they once may win the bridge,
　What hope to save the town?"

Then out spake brave Buck Watkins,
　(Who'd just arriven late),
"Now every nigger in this town
　Goes under soon or late.
And as fur as I kin see, ole hoss,
　We're facing mighty odds,
Enough tew raise a nigger's hair,
　I dew, by all the gods.

So let us go an' raise ole Cain
　About the Yankee's ears;
I bet a hoss, a shot er two
　Will make them run like deers.
In yonder place a thousand
　May well be stopped by three;
Now which of yew will step around
　An' keep the bridge with me?"

Then out there spake Hank Linton,
    A rummy'un proud was he :
" Ole coon, I guess I'll just wade in
    And keep the bridge with thee."
And out piped one-eyed Monkton.
    " I reckon I'll climb out
Of this yer ancient pow-wow house,
    An' throw some lead about."

" Buck Watkins," said the Consul,
    " I guess thet way will dew ;
So throw yer flask this way, ole cuss,
    And let me drink tew yew."
Then off they hoofed it all-fired slick,
    While folks they smole, " he, he ! "
A-thinkin' of the Yankee crowd
    Rubbed out by that 'ar three.

Now while the three were slinging
    Their rifles on their backs,
The Consul was the foremost man
    Tew take in hand an axe :
And leetle chaps and tall ones
    With tomahawk and crow,
Did smite upon the planks above
    And loose the props below.

Meanwhile the Yankee army,
  Amazin' tew behold,
Came heeling pleasantly along,
Singing a patriotic song
  Of liberty and gold.
The three defenders smole aloud,
  —A peal of warlike glee,
As that great host with measured tread,
With rifles bright and ensigns spread,
Came sailing towards the bridge's head,
  Where stood the mighty three.

The three stood calm and silent,
  And chaffed the Yankee foes ;
With one hand on the shooting iron,
  And one upon the nose.
And forth three chiefs came spurring
  Before the mighty mass ;
Tew earth they sprang, their pistols drew,
Cocked them and cussed awhile, then flew
  Tew win the narrow pass.

Warrington from Dacotah,
  A mighty man, yew bet ;
And Bowie Bill from Utah,
  The bulliest ever met ;
And Broncho Tom from Idaho,
  Who dearly loved a fight ;
And bossed a hull brigade of chaps,
With dark blue coats and scarlet caps,
Who of the whole array, perhaps,
  Were mostly always tight.

Old Linton scattered Warrington
  Into the stream beneath ;
And Monkton tackled Broncho Tom,
  And left naught but his teeth ;
At Bowie Bill brave Watkins
  Let out a mighty blow,
And that old ruffian's spirituals
  Were took in charge below.

Then Dock O'Neale from Michigan,
  Went fur the gallant three ;
And Hunt of Pennsylvania,
  —A mighty man was he ;
And Tommy Potts from Wyoming,
  Who laid out Jimmy Tupp ;
Road Agent Tupp who had his men
  Amidst the reeds of Tahoe's fen,
And put up coaches until when
  Pott's bullet curled him up.

Hank Linton rubbed out Tommy ;
  Monkton laid low O'Neale ;
Buck's bullet went right bang through Hunt,
  And made him yell and squeal.
Another bullet sent him
  Tew Bowie Bill, beneath ;
" No more," cried Buck, "you'll loaf around,
An ornament on this yer ground : "
And then a sulphureous sound
  Came bounding through his teeth.

But now no yells of triumph
    Were heard among the foes;
Though Monkton's eyes were badly blacked,
    And smashed was Linton's nose.
Six gun's lengths from this playground
    Halted the Yankee show,
And fur a space no feller stirred,
    —Funky? Lor' bless me, no!

But hark! the cry is "Burnley!"
    And, lo! the ranks divide,
And the Governor of Oregon
    Comes with his stately stride.
Upon his ample shoulders
    The epaulets they shine,
And in his hand the shooting iron,
    Tew use which he does pine.

He smole at those bold fellers,
    A smile serene and high;
And he sneered at his companions
    'Till they felt inclined to cry.
Quoth he, "these catawampi
    Stand savagely at bay;
But will ye dare tew foller,
    If Burnley leads the way?"

Then raising up his pistol,
    He 'lowed he'd start the fuss ;
And a bullet winged its way tew Buck,
    But he, the wily cuss,
With oaths and various cuss-words
    Right deftly turned the blow.
The blow, though turned, came mighty nigh,
It missed his snout, but ripped his thigh ;
The Yankees raised a joyful cry
    Tew see the red blood flow.

He reeled, and right on Linton,
    He leaned fur jest a space ;
Then like a catamount thet's riz
    He went fur Burnley's face.
Through teeth and skull, etcetera,
    So fierce a blow he sped,
That when they gathered up the corpse,
    They couldn't find the head.

And the great lordly Yankee
    Fell at thet deadly stroke,
As falls on poor humanity
    A badly laboured joke.
With crashing and with dire effect
    It lies all strewn around,
And the folks groan and mutter,
    And make a mournful sound.

On Burnley's chest Buck Watkins
  Right gleefully did dance;
And both his pards on either side
  Did jump around and prance.
"And see," cried Buck, "the welcome
  That waits yew fellers here!
What noble Yankee boy comes next
  Tew taste our Southern cheer?"

But at his joyful war-whoop
  A sullen murmur ran,
Composed of cuss-words and of oaths,
  Along the Yankee van.
There lacked not men of courage,
  Or things like that yew know;
For all the Yank nobility
  Were round the fatal show.

But all the Yank nobility's
  Hearts fell intew their boots,
Fur they didn't suffer keenly
  Tew join in such disputes;
And from the gory playground,
  Where those three mighties stood,
All shrank, like boys who try tew hook
Candy; are caught and brought tew book,
And picked up by the neck and shook
Out of their skins when outraged cook
  Catches them, as she should.

None keered tew be the foremost
   Tew lead such dire attack ;
Fur those behind cried "sail ahead !"
   And those in front cried "back !"
And backward and now forward
   Palpitates the array,
And all the fellers standing there
Began tew cuss and pull their hair,
Fire their revolvers, rip and tear,
   And wish tew go away.

Meanwhile the other fellers
   Hev worked jest like the deuce,
And helped tew raise the river
   With streams of baccy juice.
"Kum, hump yerself, Buck Watkins !"
   Cried loud the fellers all,
"Back, Linton ; put out, Monkton ;
   The darned thing's goin' ter fall."

Then Linton legged it over,
   And Monkton streaked it back ;
And as they passed, beneath their boots
   They felt the timbers crack.
But when they turned their phisogs,
   And on the farther shore
Saw brave Buck Watkins standing,
   They would hev crossed once more.

But like a Texas Norther
  Fell every loosened beam ;
And like a dam the planks and things
  Lay plumb across the stream.
And a long yell of triumph
  Rose from the Southern bank ;
As every stay was washed away,
  And all the irons sank.

Alone stood brave Buck Watkins,
  And thought it was unkind
Fur both his pards tew make their tracks
  And leave him thar behind.
A shot his leg hed broken,
  He couldn't stir a prop ;
The Yankees yelled tew him tew yield,
  Or him they'd surely drop.

Round turned he, with his nose turned up,
  Which riled them much tew see ;
And shouted to the fellers
  Tew throw a rope tew he.
Right then a Yankee soldier
  Jest shoved him in the back :
He made things hum, and scrambled sum,
  And in the stream went whack,

A lasso from the Southern bank
   Encircled round his head,
And luckless Watkins really guessed
   Thet he'd be choked tew dead.
Fur the current ran like sixty,
   And with his broken prop
He couldn't struggle muchly,
   And tried tew holler "stop!"

Yew bet your boots, no swimmer,
   In such a darned affair,
Struggled through such a scrimmage,
   And came out with his hair.
But his limbs were borne up mainly
   By the shallow river bed,
And also the riata,
   Which grappled with his head.

And now they reach out fur him,
   Tew catch him by the hair,
And every one comes crowding
   Tew hev their fill of stare.
And when at last they scoop him up,
   Tew all-fired weak tew stir,
They hear him cry "How's thet fur high;
   I guess we raised sum hair."

DIED IN HIS BOOTS.

HE smoke of battle lay around,
        Men, dead and wounded, strewed the ground,
            And we, the Rangers, saw
Our troops victorious on thet field,
And still the Yankees would not yield,
    But came fur one charge more.

Right through the smoke ahead, a sound
Thet caused our hearts to madly bound,
    Broke quick and suddenly ;
A trumpet pealing loud and shrill,
And charging straight upon our hill
    The Union cavalry

Came swooping.   Quick the order runs,
" Now then, my boys, stand to your guns,
    And give the Yankees H——l."
Our rifles cracked with one report,
And stopped those charging horsemen short,
    And many of them fell.

But still a few came rushing on
Our very bayonets upon,
    Which soon their ardour quenched.
But one poor fellow in this check
Hed got a hole made in his neck,
    —With blood his clothes were drenched.

We dragged him in, but nearly dead,
The jugular was severëd,
  His life was flowing fast.
One of us in the ragged wound
His finger thrust, and then he found
  It stopped the flow at last.

" Sonny," the Ranger gently said,
" When I remove my claw you're dead,
  So if you hev a friend,
Jest write a line er tew, ter say
How you got rubbed out in the fray,
  An' it tew him I'll send."

The soldier looked his thanks tew him,
And, as his eyes began to swim,
  Unto his mother he
A few last words of greeting sent,
And then, his strength all being spent,
  He looked up quietly :

An' tew the Ranger said, " Ole hoss
Let it go now ; an' thank yew, boss ;"
  The Ranger drew his hand.
The spouting blood in jets poured forth,
And with one look towards the North,
  He struck the Better Land.

A WAIL FROM OLD YURRUP.

H, once a little sportsman, boys,
    Did raise a little house,
  In little England, fur he 'lowed
He'd shoot sum little grouse.

But ah, my boys, thet little land
    Is full of little laws ;
So when thet little man pitched in,
    'Twas fur thet little cause

Thet all the little grouse were not
    A little scarcer made,
When little sportsman went abroad
    Tew make his little raid.

Great Scott ! 'twas fun ; thet little man
    He little thought that he
Was by a little Britisher
    Watched through a little tree.

A little while he loafed around,
    Until a little board
His little-interested gaze
    A little time absorbed.

He'as not a little bit put out
　Tew read the little bill,
Which said in little pithy words
　Thet little grouse tew kill

Was not considered little crime
　By little sportsman there,
And added little nasty threats
　Tew raise one's little hair.

Thet little man he lighted out
　In mighty little time ;
And when in little Yankee-land,
　Composed this little rhyme.

But little while before he left,
　A little sum he paid
Tew thet thar little Britisher
　Fur his one little raid.

And now he thinks thet little land
　Tew little fellers he
Will leave a little while and live
　In little 'Meriky.

NATURE.

HOW beautiful is Nature, undefiled,
  And viewed in all its native loveliness !
    The beauteous tints of early spring, the warm
Rich beauty of the summer; then, in turn,
The gorgeous autumn with its varied tints,
And winter with its coverlet of snow.
The morning, and the bright warm day; the night;
Brings each its sense of harmony to man;
And teaches him of One celestial God
Almighty.
        When the darkness of the night
Is over, and above the distant hills
The glorious sun uprises, then are seen
Soft gentle tints and bold sharp outlines blent
In perfect beauty, just as when our earth,
Fresh from the hand of God, created stood
Till man was made, to have dominion o'er
The hills and trees, rivers and living things—
And then commenced destruction.   But till then
All was in harmony.   No wars or strifes
Joyful to human nature; all was peace.
The mountains rise precipitous from earth
Like some strong man, who looketh up as though
To pierce the veil that separates ourselves
From Heaven : and the bright sun pours his rays
O'er hill and vale, mountain and sleeping lake.

Down in the valleys, full of lovely flowers,
Rise the soft mists when the first sunbeam bids
The earth awaken to another day ;
Among the trees the songs of birds arise
To greet the glorious sun, and scene by scene
Comes from the shadows as the sunbeams pierce
The darkness, and array the world in light :
The distant peaks in many-coloured hues
Rise boldly from the mists, and beauty add
To beauteous scene ; and light and gauzy clouds
Float overhead, tinted in blue and gold.
The rivulet that down the mountain pours,
Catches the smiling beams, and smiles returns
As though in thanks ; for everything gives thanks
Excepting man, who always strives for more
Than what he has.   The rainbow that above
The waterfall for ever hovers, when
The bright beams glance upon the dancing spray,
Shines brilliantly in all its gorgeous wealth
Of tinted beauty, as the streams of light
Pour through the trees to gaze upon the depths
Of gloomy cañon where the river runs
Tumultuous.
         The lake, amidst the woods
Like diamond set in emeralds, reclines,
Fed by the mountain streams that downward rush
From where, among the many tinted clouds,
The everlasting hills uplift their heads ;
Which are to man fit emblems of the great
Imperishable majesty of God.

Such emblems the untutored savage sees,
And learns in love what civilisëd men
Learn by far harder means, if learn at all.
And see! the limpid wave like mirror shows
The gay reflection of the sunlit sky;
And down within its bright transparent depths
The fishes dart about, and flash their scales
Like molten gold and silver as they rush
In sportive play among the water reeds.
The swallows, on their pointed pinions skim
The bright clear surface of the glassy lake
In chase of insect prey; the ripples spread,
Increasing o'er the surface as they dip
Their spotless breasts within the cooling stream,
And then uprise in swift and sudden flight,
And swoop again, and with shrill joyous cries
Continue on their meteoric flight.
Far from the earth against the azure sky
Is seen the great war-eagle, sailing slow
Around in circles, gazing for his prey,
And sudden pouncing, like the bolt from heaven,
Upon defenceless kid; for 'tis a law
Of God for beasts on other beasts to prey,
That they might not too mightily increase.
Upon the plain the antelopes abound,
Fleet, lovely creatures, living out their days
In happiness, and free from every care,
Rejoicing in their nature.
                 Look around!
What change has taken place in the bright scene?

What means this sudden gloom?   Down from the north
Comes a black cloud, intensely black, wherefrom
Sharp pointed flashes of electric light
Go crackling through the gloomy vault of Heaven.
Short gusts of wind now come, and thund'rous roars
Rolling through space infinite, and the rain
Pours from the clouds in torrents.   Frightened birds
Fly swiftly to the shelter of the woods,
And Nature cowers beneath the fury of
The elements.   Through the grim cañon's depths
The lightning flashes blindingly and oft,
Illuminating those dark cavernous spots
As by the light of day, and from the stern
Dark adamantine mountains echoes roll
Unceasing, as the thunder through the sky
Goes sonorous rolling, and the mighty wind
Sweeps o'er the forest with tremendous strength.
Tall lusty oaks go crashing down before
Its power irresistible, and leaves
Fly through the air, and boughs and sticks bestrew
The moistened ground.   So sweep through human souls
The storms of passion, but to Nature's storms
Holding reversëd meaning, for the one
Teacheth Almighty Power, the other but
Shows mankind's weakness to resist the power
Of Satan.   Thus is Nature.   Watch her well.

HUMANUM EST.

LL that people work for here,
        And the cost is mighty dear,
            Is three little letters—£ s. d.;
They slave both day and night
With all their main and might,
    And the reason why I cannot wholly see.

Folks work until they drop,
And then they will not stop,
    But still go fighting desperately ;
And when they've made their pile
They still want to strike ile,
    And to rope in more of £ s. d.

They never give a thought
To salvation, as they ought,
    But go through life most recklessly ;
But they'll find to their dismay,
When they come to the Last Day,
    That they'll have too much of Hell.

                                    S. D.

GONE UNDER.

 TRAPPERS' rendezvous on Southern Platte ;
    A joyous meet of friends long rent asunder ;
    A few familiar faces missing there ;
  Some questionings ; the sure reply—gone under.

Gone under. What conjectures shape themselves
  Of the poor trapper whose life-blood is shed
By ruthless savages, when day is done
  And he reclines in peace upon his bed.

A shot—a shriek—the earthly drama over,
  And no kind friend to stand around and wonder
Where is the soul of that lone trapper now,
  Who's gone to join the multitude gone under ?

But all is merry where companions meet,
  And little thought they give unto the morrow,
But drink and gamble, smoke and count their coups,
  And cast away all trace of pain and sorrow.

The dice is thrown, the cup goes round, and gamblers
  Round the rough tables gather in the plunder ;
Disputes arise, guns flash and bowies glisten,
  And, slain by their companions, more go under.

And so they go ; those poor brave reckless trappers,
  Fighting their way through life till some sad blunder
Causes their death. Next rendezvous the question
  "Hullo, whar's Tom ?" Reply, " Dunno,—gone under."

D. BOONE.

HE Policeman rode behind a van,
    When he the fight began to scan,
    That he his courage (?) might arrange—
He badly wished his clothes to change ;
Alone he rode—from head to heel
A sorter funk that boy could feel :
Not mounted he on war-horse white,
But brown, for so that in a fight
He'd not be a too conspicuous sight :
A helmet brave of blue was set
Upon his head with anguish wet ;
And tied on with a piece of twine
Was seen A1 in figures fine :
Courage, or aught like it, he lacks,
Bearing that ancient motto *Pax.*

He saw the fellows have their fight
Right in the road in open sight,
They banged and thumped away right sore.
Having an up and down young war ;
Then rested on their feet awhile,
Lest they their clothes with blood should s'ile,
And hold high counsel, if that night
Should close the strife or morning light—
For both the combatants were tight.
Oh, gay, yet fearful to behold,
The position of that bobby bold,
For suddenly that coon was sold,
—*The wagon rolled away.*

And who, that saw that policeman ride,
Could ever think of him defied,
Or could his direful doom foretell,
Or think of him so soon in Spain ;
For in his wavering eye was set
A little tear all moist and wet.
When all the niggers at a glance
Saw him, he wished he was in France.
" Say, Bill," said one, " you know of course
Who's him that's sitting on that horse ? "
" The tokens on his helmet tell,
A1, old hoss, I know him well."
And shall that cheeky bobby brave
Our presence ? What a saucy knave !
" I guess," said one unholy sot,
" If I'd a sword like one he's got,
To give him beans and make him sick,
By Jove, I'd even use a stick."
" On this yer day," William replied,
" Nice fencing rules are set aside ;
Still will the bobby dare our wrath ?
You on that hoss, just clear the path ! "
And at the ranger's signal, soon
Dashed at the bob. young Dannie Boone.

Of ancient backwood's blood he came,
A race renowned for Injun fame ;
He burned, before the ranger's eye
To do some deed of chivalry ;
He spurred his horse, he raised his stick,
And like a flash he went off slick.

Quite motionless with funk and fear,
And feeling all was ending here,
The bob. stood fast, and thought "Oh dear!"
While down on him like flash of flame,
Spurring full pelt the cowboy came.
The blue-bird may the eagle mock,
If poor old bobby stand the shock ;
For in the cowboy's mad career,
Half dead with funk, and quite with fear,
His corpse was scattered on the floor,
And poor A1's career was o'er.
High in the stirrups stood the boy,
And whooped aloud with pride and joy ;
Then all the crowd went off to drink,
And thus their troubles all to sink.

NIGHT.

IGHT on the Prairie. A perfect calm
  Sinks upon nature ; save the summer breeze
  Whispering soft 'midst grass and sleeping flowers.
Above, the dark blue canopy, wherein
Rideth the silvery moon, whose soft, bright light,
Dark moving shadows, and mysterious, casts
Upon the sleeping plain, when midnight clouds
Float through the Heavens, and obstruct her path.
A very Paradise of solitude. A deep,
Soft consciousness of that almighty love
Flowing from Heaven unto sinful Earth,
Subduing. So serenely glides the night.

   * * * * *

Night in the Forest. Full of joyous life ;
Mysterious flitting shadows ; tiny lights
As borne by fairies ; glancing--disappear
To flash again in dark recesses, and
Illuminate the night. Shrill, distant notes,
And low, soft murmurs near and all around ;
The thousand voices of the summer night,
Soft, bell-like, thrilling, steal upon the ear
Of midnight wanderer in the forest glades.
The noiseless flitting bats and soft winged birds
Of night, on downy pinions quick pursue
Their insect prey, with sharp and thrilling cries.

The moon's bright beams fall through the leafy boughs
 Of cottonwood and wild acacia, and
The tangled underbrush of ages.　They
Black shadows cast, and flitting, as the breeze
Soft wafting o'er the calm, serene expanse
Of verdure, stirs a myriad sleeping leaves,
And passes on.　The soft, subduing spell
Cast by the night o'er nature, rules supreme.

A GREAT TIME.

 SAT me down to write a poem
　　But couldn't get inspired :
　　I thought, and thought, and thought again,
　And ditto, till I's tired :
I couldn't scare up any theme
　I thought would be admired.

Several appeared unto this child,
　But none of them would shine :
I thought I'd write of Pontiac,
　Or Bingen on the Rhine :
I sat and thought from six o'clock
　Until it happened nine.

I couldn't think, to save my life,
　Of anything at all :
I looked up at the ceiling,
　And downward at the wall.
The silence reigned so utterly
　I heard me growing tall.

To make it worse, 'twas Summer time,
　At least 'twas in July ;
I'm of that fuming, wretched set
　Who never can keep dry :
And sitting thinking there like that
　Was not the way to try.

At last I guess I went to sleep,
  For suddenly I heard
A noise I'd never seen before,
  It felt just like a bird;
And things got kinder jumbled up—
  It really was absurd.

I heard a chap " Good Morning " say,
  And " Have you used Pears' Soap ?
It's a grateful morning beverage
  Beloved of the Pope."
Another said, " No, Epps's best,
  That you'll admit, I hope."

And then I heard another voice
  Say, " Coleman's Mustard is
The best Tobacco to be smoked
  At play or during biz.,
It wont wash clothes !" at which untruth
  My dander fairly riz.

Then Hudson's Soap and Ivy Soap
  And Brookes's took the stage :
They each were better than the rest,
  It made me in a rage
To hear about an antidote
  Against the march of age.

And then a chap as bald as sin
  With Hair Renewer came;
He said because that he was bald
  His stuff was not to blame:
It was most unsurpassëd for
  The speechless, halt and maim.

Then Keen his Mustard brought along
  And said 'twas far the best;
And Colman he had better go
  To——no, it wasn't West.
(I made a note I'd get them both,
  And put them to the test.)

And then a chap in tones polite
  " Good Morning, Sir," said he ;
" Have you your Bovril had? 'Tis good
  For Saving Life at Sea."
Another said, " Yes, but I find
  That Cleaver's Soap is THE."

I heard that filtered water's best,
  But Pluralis is better;
It's cooling, more thirst-quenching and
  Immeasurably wetter :
But patent Telephones are best
  For copying a letter.

At last this half-bred poet woke,
    And thought these things were some ;
But wondered how they got mixed up
    So horribully rum:
And really such a thing could not
    Be very well kept mum.

P.S.—I've tried the mustards C. and K.,
    But which does take the cake
I will not say, for I should not
    Impression like to make
That I am advertising for
    The filthy lucre's sake.

SAM BLACKBURN'S RIDE.

ICTORIO'S raided the border line at the head of his
Indian braves,
   From Albuquerque to where the flag above Fort
   Leaton waves :
And pressing hard upon his heels the Texas Rangers go,
They chased his band from the Rio Grande down into Mexico.
They have passed the smoking ruins on their swift avenging track
Which the Chief has made in his flying raid and left behind
   his back ;
And little children dying, and women left to mourn
A husband, or son, or brother—someone from whom the scalp
   is torn.
They have looked on those bloody traces, and cursed the
   ruthless foe,
And ridden amain with a loosened rein till they came to Durango :
And there they have lost the Indian trail, nor searching brought
   to light
The track of the man in th' Apaché van, whom they fondly
   thought in sight.
And Blackburn hath wheeled his Rangers back, and sworn by
   fire and flood
Though 'twere Satan he met in an Indian guise, he would have
   that Indian's blood.
They have ridden back to the Rio Grande and camped 'midst
   the rocks and trees,
To rest them after their long, hard ride, in the cool of the
   evening breeze :

And they squat in groups around the fires, and lay upon the
  grass,
And smoke their pipes 'neath the darkening sky in a cañon of
  The Pass.
Sam Blackburn sat away from them with blackness in his heart,
For he had not met a foeman yet, and so he sat apart
And smoked his pipe in solitude and then lay down to sleep;
His men lay down as well and soon were wrapped in slumber
  deep.
The Ranger awoke at midnight, and leaped up with a start,
His hair uprose upon his head, and wildly beat his heart:
With startled glance he looked askance, to see if all was right;
The Rangers all were wrapped in sleep, the fires were flickering
  bright:
And on his gun the sentry leaned like statue carved from wood,
Watchful and vigilant; and around, the horses, grazing, stood.
The Ranger Chief rose silently and went from among the trees,
And he saw a sight in the bright moonlight that caused his
  blood to freeze.
'Twas strange 'twas so, for there he saw what he had wished
  to see—
An Indian brave, one of the band he had chased so bitterly.
And yet he felt an awesome fear as he gazed at the warrior
  there—
He seemed, to the Ranger's eyes, to glow with a phosphorescent
  glare:
And he cast no midnight shadow on the waving prairie flowers.
But seemed to float in the quiet air, in the mystic, dark, night-
  hours:

And the night-winds gathered around him with a strange
    unearthly sound,
And pale blue lightning seemed to flash and wrap the Shape
    around.
The Ranger feared no earthly foe, but, gracious Heavens! this
    Thing,
Mounted on horse with flaming eyes and black as the raven's
    wing,
With hoofs that touched not solid earth, were enough to fill
    with fright
Whoever chanced to happen there and view the fearsome sight.
Sam trembled, and he turned to flee, but his limbs to move
    were loath,
And the voice of the Phantom cried to him—" Remember this
    thine oath :
" ' By the waters of Heaven and fires of Hell, if Indian I shall
    meet,
" ' Though twere Satan himself in Indian guise, I will lay him
    dead at my feet ;'
" And bethinkest thou, O mortal man, who in unthought hath
    grown,
" 'Twere a daring and a fearful thing to jest upon things
    unknown!"
And the Ranger hath turned with a cry to Heaven to help him
    in his need,
And dauntlessly faced the Infernal Man astride the Infernal Steed.
" If my horse were here," he said aloud, " by my vow that I
    have sworn,
" I'd chase that Red," the Ranger said, " though it be till the
    Judgment Dawn!"

A wondrous wind of a sudden blew, and Blackburn gasped for
    breath ;

He saw in an instant lightning-flash the Unknown Place of
    Death !

And now he was seated astride his horse, and out in the moon-
    light bright,

On the grassy steppes 'bove the cañon's depths, which yawned
    upon his right :

And in front of him the Indian Chief, sitting upon his steed ;

An earthly form—yet not of earth : a mystery indeed.

Upon his head, tip-stained with red, the eagle-plumes waved
    free,

And either side the horns that told of Satan's majesty :

And the soft dressed hide of the buffalo hung gracefully
    and low,

And underneath, the arrow-sheath, with arrows and a bow.

The Chief's black hair flowed o'er the robe, and swept his
    charger's flanks,

Shining with fat of beaver from the Colorado's banks.

And around his neck the horrid claws of monstrous grizzly
    bears—

Proud ornament, proclaiming that the wearer knows no fears.

And around his waist a mighty belt with tomahawk and knife,

And bead-decked leggings fringed with scalps, each answering
    for a life ;

Telling of slaughtered champions, and prowess grim and bold ;

Adornment meet for a mighty chief, but dreadful to behold.

The steed was worthy of the man he bore upon his back,

Whate'er a horse should be, he was, nor anything did lack :

A proud, arched crest and mighty chest, round eye, red nostril
spread,

Full flowing mane and tail, fine limbs, and cameo-clear shaped
head.

A glorious steed caparisoned and decked with Indian pride,

With floating plumes and bead-worked straps, and cyncha bold
and wide.

And the Ranger's eye glanced longingly at that unearthly beast,

He almost wished to make it his, and still the wish increased.

And the Rider hath looked into Blackburn's eyes, and there
hath found no fear,

And he said " Thou hast uttered a foolish thing, that has caused
my presence here.

" But if thou hast courage to face those things that should not
be known of thee,

" I will show thee how to perform the oath that thou sweared
so thoughtlessly."

And Blackburn hath answered the Phantom's speech with scorn
and frightful mirth,

" A Chief of the Texas Rangers fears no thing in Hell or Earth!"

" A reckless man is he who can thus jest," the Shadow said,

" Now listen to my terms and see to what thy vow hath led."

And to him he disclosed the name of the Prince of the Lower
Spheres,

And the Ranger quaked at the sound of it, and his mind was
filled with fears.

" And hark to me," the Devil said, " to thy steed I give the power

" To run—not more fleet than he now can run—but to run hour
after hour

" Without fatigue or want of breath ; and thou shalt ride amain
" The present night till to-morrow's light dies out and night
     comes again ;
" And chase me till we reach the hills and crags of the Rocky
     Mountains,
" To the waters of the Yellowstone, and to the ink-black fountains
" Eustis and Biddle : furthermore, by the mighty name I hold,
" I swear to thee, if o'erta'en I be by thy courage and riding bold,
" Thou shalt find an Indian brave indeed, mounted upon this
     horse,
" Whom thou shalt prevail against and slay, and keep thy vow
     by force.
" And if thou winnest in this race, I grant to thee the steed,
" He shall serve to thee, and unequalled be for courage and for
     speed.
" But if thou losest, when we come to the mystic lakes of mine
" Thou shalt go with me to the Unknown Place, where perchance
     are kin of thine.
" I will trust to thee to fulfil thy word, for thou art what a man
     should be :
" And now, O mortal, acceptest thou the terms laid down by me?"
Sam looked at the steed, and he made his mind to keep his vow
     or go
With the Spirit Enemy of his race to the Unknown Place below :
And he longed for the horse that he might obtain—'twas as fair
     as a horse could be ;
And the Ranger hath sworn with a terrible oath—" I take the
     terms of thee !"

And his sharp spurs sank in his mustang's flank, and he shot
like an arrow from bow
Towards the Satanic Indian Chief, hoping to take him so.
But the Devil hath turned in a flash of flame, and hied him
through the grass,
And the night-air whistled round Blackburn's form as he galloped
from The Pass.
And evil bats and wondrous birds went wheeling all around,
And the phosphorescent flashes flew and died upon the ground :
And the tail of the black horse in his front like cloud of thunder
flowed,
And wondrous Things accompanied them, and whirlwinds round
them blowed.
The miles flew by and fell behind, unheeded in the chase,
And the mustang flew, and the black horse flew, urged on in the
dreadful race.
All night was the fearful speed kept up, till the flash of the
morning grey,
O'er mountains and hills and flowing rills, till they came to
Santa Fé.
And men, amazed and wondering, looked, to see the Ranger fly,
For they could not see that Form in front that he chased so
earnestly.
Taos is reached and left behind, and the Colorado line
Is reached and passed, and just as fast speed the two chargers fine.
And Spanish peaks are left behind like marvels of a dream,
Pike's Peak and Denver City passed in the bright sunlight's gleam.
And when an obstacle was reached Sam deemed might not be
passed,
It disappeared, and all was plain, and so was reached at last

Cheyenne, the town of Wyoming, and still Sam Blackburn kept
In tempting touch of the raven horse as swiftly on they lept.
And the Rider hath looked him back in awe to see his foe so
    near,
And his charger flew to'ards the hills of blue, where lay the
    Lakes of Fear.
The Ranger's teeth are shut like iron, and his veins are like
    knotted ropes, ·
As he sees on the far horizon's bar the goal of all his hopes.
And the Lakes are in sight! . . . . And they pitch and
    boil! And shadowy vampires fly
From the dreadful depths of the ink-black pools to watch the
    chase go by.
And horrid forms flit noiselessly through upper voids of space,
And the black horse snorts flame and rolling smoke as he flies
    on his losing race!
The Ranger hath need of his courage now in this whirlwind
    not of earth,
Surrounded by dreadful forms and shapes that laugh in hideous
    mirth:
And he hath cried in his dire distress on the Name of the
    Lord of Life
To aid him in this his fearful need, and to help him in the
    strife:
And a figure is floating by his side, wondrous and fair to see—
An Angel bright with radiant light and Heavenly majesty.
And as he gazed in gratitude on this beauteous sign of grace,
He knew, with a thrill of love and joy, 'twas his Mother's form
    and face.

She had prayed the Almighty to give her leave to help her son
in need,
And hath winged her way from the Spirit Land with the fiery
meteor's speed.
And the hideous forms of the evil things have melted and
shrunk away,
Like as the fogs of autumn shrink from the glorious sunbeam's ray.
And the Spirit hath seized the mustang's rein, and to urge him
fleeter tries,
And the Ranger rides in touch of the Brave, who turns and
looks in his eyes :
" Bethinkest thou," he cried to Sam, with a smile of pity and glee,
" The word of the Prince of Deceit is worth the word of true
man like thee ?
" Thou hast pressed me harder than man before, but for nought
are all thy pains ! "
And Blackburn called on his Mother's name, and shook his
mustang's reins,
And is up to the·tail of the Devil's horse as he reaches the
black lake's strand,
And bends from the saddle and catches the tail in the grasp of
his strong right hand.
A downward jerk round the hinder leg, and the black horse
falls on his flank
With a crash like the storm-bolt's horrid noise, and in the
black pool he sank.
And a dismal smoke filled all the place, and the pale blue
lightning flared,
And rushing winds went wailing by, and the fires of phosphorous
glared.

But a sweet voice came from the gloom :—" My son, thou'rt
    safe now as before,
" But beware how thou makest thy future vows, for I may not
    aid thee more."
And then, with a parting kiss of love, his Mother's spirit fled,
And Blackburn, trembling at all these things, hath turned his
    horse's head
For to flee from that Devil-haunted place; and when he had
    ridden afar,
He dismounted, and on his bended knees he thanked the Lord
    in prayer
For the kindly help vouchsafed him through his loved Mother's
    aid ;
And that her spirit might guide him till they meet again, he
    prayed.
He rode him back to the Rio Grande, and his men were still
    asleep,
Just as he left them, encampèd at the foot of the cañon steep :
For the dreadful power of Satan had caused this thing to be ;
But he waked them up, and they lit the fires and feasted merrily.
And in after times the Ranger Chief avenged the settlers' wrongs,
For his mustang's powers were themes for tales and for rough
    Border songs :
But to no one he told of his fearful ride to fulfil the vow he made,
And a better life he has led from that time when the Devil's
    plan was stayed.

But beware how thou makest thy future vows.

PAINTING THE TOWN RED.

 HOOP! crash!! bang!!! yell!!!! "Stand aside!
　　Step right into this saloon :
What's the circus all about?
　　Wal, I 'low you'll find out soon.

"San Antonio's the diggins
　　On the Fourth July, I 'low,
Ef you suffer to discover
　　What's the meaning of pow-wow.

" Here's some cowboys from the plains,—
　　Ever see a madder crowd?
You can bet your bottom dollar
　　They'll make things look kinder loud."

In a line, at furious gallop,
　　Dash the mustangs through the town ;
Glimpse of red shirts, high-fringed leggins,
　　Long black hair and faces brown.

Whoop ! revolvers flash and crackle—
　　Clouds of dust and neigh of steed ;
High-peaked saddles, swinging lassos—
　　How they ride !　What reckless speed !

" Look, thar's Buck ; he fit the Injuns
    Down at Horse-Shoe, week ago ;
See him swinging his riata—
    Spiling for sum fun I 'low."

Here's a thirsty heap of fellows
    Charging to the tavern door ;
Throw their horses to their haunches—
    Leap to earth, and " take the floor."

Hank cries : " Boys, it's my treat this turn,
    Don't be bashful, call yer drink;"
" Gin sling," " stone wall," " corpse reviver,"
    Put down 'fore you've time to wink.

Mount and off again, and dashing
    Headlong, firing in the air :
Boisterous mirth's abroad this fête-day,
    View of Pandemonium rare.

" See thet Chinaman out yonder?
    Guess he'd better stir his peg ;
Silly cuss !   I thought so ! Weston's
    Roped him round the off hind leg.

" Hear the war-whoop ? Now they're at it !
    Full of whisky—ripe for fights :
You kin gamble on it, stranger,
    Thet you'll see some proper sights."

In the throng a drunken "Greaser"
  Shoots a cowboy; what a noise!
" Darn them Mexikins!" "Let's shoot him!"
  " Rope him!" "Stab him!" "Lynch him, boys!"

Soon the frightened wretch is collared,
  Strung up to a signpost tall:
Someone shoots the rope asunder—
  Down the vaquero does fall.

Party feeling's now awakened,
  Vaqueros came charging down;
And the war-whoop's loudest echoes
  Summon aid throughout the town.

" Here's the Sheriff and his fellers!"
  Sudden order for a space:
Three boys taken to the prison,
  There the penalty to face.

Evening comes, the fun grows madder
  (If that's possible to be);
Bullets fly in all directions,
  But we're used to that, you see.

Bonfires blaze, and fireworks crackle;
  Round them, mounted and on foot,
Cowboys, Trappers, "Greasers," Injuns,
  Grimed with powder, dust and soot.

Reckless charges, savage yellings,
　　Make the wooden buildings shake :
Such a row !　Enough to make a
　　" Down East " tenderfoot to quake.

Up the steps of a " Posada,"
　　Mad with drink a cowboy spurs ;
And the little mustang gamely
　　Scrambles up the wooden stairs.

Quick stampede among the fellows,
　　" Now you niggers, cl'ar the bar ! "
Out revolvers—lively scrimmage—
　　Out go lamps—great times right thar.

Cowboy gets a bullet in him,
　　Lights out for the door again :
Pony jumps the steps, and charges
　　Down the street araising Cain.

Whoopings, yellings, shots from pistols,
　　Maddest capers, all are there ;
Now the boys are full of whisky
　　Better look out for your hair.

" Here's a hoss without a rider ! "
　　" Stop him ! " " Rope him ! " " Throw him down ! "
Twenty boys with swinging lassos
　　Chase the pony through the town.

" Whoop ! Hooray ! Jest cl'ar the gangway ! "
  " Someone down ! " " Oh, never mind,"
Wheel, and swoop, and rush, and clatter—
  Every care thrown to the wind.

" Guess we'll put back for the Rancho ;
  Mount your hoss and follow slick.
Mind thet lasso ! Duck yer head, thar !
  Ah ! out bowie, cut it quick !

" Stopped a bullet ? Never mind, hoss ;
  Here's the outskirts of the town :
Here's the prairie ; now we'll hump it,
  Leave the boys to prance around."

You can bet your bottom dollar
  That no other time can show,
As the Fourth July, such doings
  Down in San Antonio.

THE GHOST DANCE OF THE INDIAN NATIONS.

WAKE! To arms! children of Uncas, rise!
   Messiah comes! our long-expected Chief,
   To lead his warriors to a final chance
To gain possession of their fathers' land.
Prepare yourselves again for vengeful strife!
Paint ye the war-post, let the war drum sound
To call the nations from afar and near :
Dig up the buried hatchet that too long
Has hidden lain beneath thy conquered soil :
Put ye on war paint, and upon your heads
The bonnet with its waving eagle plumes.
Deck ye your mustangs in the pride of war :
Bring forth the long sharp lance and feathered shaft—
The weapons of your fathers, who, perchance,
Watch with their spirit eyes, with impotent,
But burning and immeasurable, desires,
This, the last effort of their fallen race.
The last! Arise! Be strong for what may come.
Up! Get together in your mystic dance,
Cry to your gods to wake and aid your cause ;
Call on your fathers from the dead to rise,
Armed with reality of legends brave,
To help their children in their last great strife—
Their strife for liberty or death.   Sing ye
Your old traditions, glorious and gone ;
Sing ye the story of your nations' wrongs ;
The broken treaties, massacres and thefts,
The long, long, memories of th'unburied past :

Pressed hard by murderous foes and baleful friends,
By gods deserted, all your heroes slain—
O, direful night of sorrow and disgrace !

Up ! Quit yourselves like men, the war drum sounds !
That sound your fathers heard when to their wilds
Immeasurable came the white men first
—O, direful advent ! And they leaped like hounds
Upon the trail, and many a gory scalp—
Triumphant trophy ! dried in Indian smoke.
But for each white man slain, three white men rose,
And by their cunning arts did so prevail,
That the red warriors sullenly retired
Before a foe so terrible and great:
But not unnoticed ! many a scalpless head
Marked each receding step, where fought the great
Powhatten, and where Uncas led his braves
To bloody victory.   Then Chingachgook fought,
And Pukeshinwa, bravest of the brave,
And Athanase and Miantonomoh :
And Pontiac led the tribes before Detroit—
Ottawa braves, and painted Chippewas ;
And but for treachery in his camp, had ta'en
The lake-side citadel :
And th'Apaché braves under Victorio rode
To many a scalp-upraising.   Mexico
Can tell a mournful tale of savage raids—
Her warriors scattered like the chaff before
The wild onrush of Indian chivalry ;

Her towns destroyed, men scalped, and children slain,
And tender women carried off to grace
The triumph of the Indian conqueror.

But what are all the memories of the past?
Where are our warriors?   Where our leaders brave?
Where Uncas? Pukeshinwa? Pontiac?
Their life-blood flowed that they our land might save.
Their spirits cry aloud ; O make reply
And follow in their steps, and do or die !
Now rise, ye nations ! dance before your gods,
And cry aloud, that they may hear your cry.
Messiah, come !

Now let us rise, ye nations, and hasten forth to war,
And cast from us the hateful yoke that we will bear no more.
Our fathers' voices cry to us from out the misty past—
" Go ! drive these strangers from your land, and take your own
         at last :
And let my children hold their hands from internecine fray,
And gather in their weakened bands to drive the foe away."
Dig up the hatchet, O my sons, our state may not endure,
And send the secret signal round to call the tribes to war.
And tell them " Come, my brethren ! and let us make a stand,
Our fathers' spirits cry ' Go forth ! retake your native land.' "
Was it for this that Uncas died, and mighty warriors bled ?
Was it for this our fathers fought, and blood like water sped ?
Let the old wounded eagle rise, and wing again his flight
To where the starry banner flies, and once again make fight.

And let your messengers go forth, north, south, and east and west,
And fan to life the smouldering spark in every warrior's breast :
And north and south and east and west to scatter far the brand
And say "Come! drive these foemen forth from this, our
    native land.
The white man's lies are in our ears, we will not hear him more;
Rise up! ye tribes—Messiah is come to lead us forth to war."
Go to the north and tell my sons " Messiah is come at last ;
Rise for your old traditions' sake, and legends of the past.
Tribes of the Sioux, now gather ye ! Burntwoods, Oglalla braves,
Assiniboines, now gather ye ! Messiah's banner waves.
Ottawas, Shawnees, Wyandottes, come to your brother's aid,
Nez-Perce's, come to aid our cause, or e'er the chance is staid.
And you, whose valiant history has been sung from shore to shore,
Delawares! once again uplift your arms and come to war !"
Go to the south and cry aloud " Ho, nations, join the fray,
For now is come the mighty Chief who was to come some day.
Seminoles and Comanches, and you, Apache braves,
Unite your tribes and come with us, avenge your fathers' graves."
And east and west send forth the cry " Now let my children
    fight ;
Not yet may lions lay down with lambs, or red men mate with
    white.
Lo, all your glory it has gone, and but the memories stay,
For all your old traditions, rise ! and haste ye to the fray.
Cheyennes and Pawnees, Senecas, Wichitas, Blackfeet, Sioux,
Arise and help us take our neck from out this fatal noose.
The white men have our fathers' land within an iron grasp,
Let the red warriors sally forth and loose the murderous clasp.

The buffalo have disappeared before the white man's face,
And his the hand firewater gives, that brought my sons disgrace.
No longer may our state endure, one effort we will make,
Dying, our last great effort from us the yoke may shake.
The forests of America shall sound with joyous whoops,
And who is he may stand upon the war path of the Loups?
The tortoise of the Delawares shall waken from his sleep
And the warriors like a catamount upon the foe shall leap:
And all the tribes shall take the axe and hurl it at the foe,
But what the end of it may be, who is there that may know?

AT THE GOAL.

HERE is a note of music in the air,
   Once heard before;
    Far back—far back o'er Life's dark, troubled sea,
  In childhood's happy hours
  Of yore.
It brings back visions of a Summer day,
The scent of new-mown hay,
The murmur of the rivulet, the hum of bees,
The bright, warm sunshine and the songs of birds
   Among the trees;
    And the far-off blue of sky;
   The scented waving fields of clover on the slopes;
    The warm wind's sigh.
Those sunny fields have no more charms for me;
For now I die.

  * * * * * *

So far it seems—so far, far back to when
  I was a child, and played
In waving cornfields, where the whispering breeze
Rustled among the stalks and shook the flowers
Of blood-red poppies—when among the trees
  I strayed.
How clear to me
  Comes back the scene!
  The waving cornstalks, where the breezes played
  And whispered wild, bright fancies. There
   I heard that note of music.

Whence had strayed
    That sound of Heaven? That wonderful pure note
    That breathed unutterable words of earth,
    And seemed to float
    'Twixt earth and Heaven, and melt away in space.
I did not dare
    To watch its flight. At close of day
I found the soul of my best-loved had passed away.

    *   *   *   *   *   *

What are these long, long years gone by
    To those to come:
I would not tread again that path of sorrow,
Despite bright, beauteous moments, when the sun
Broke through thick clouds of horror.
    I see a face!
There's one has waited long for me,
Whose touch is on my hand to bid me come:
I see the Glory!

LET SLEEPING DOGS LIE.

OW there lived in Carolina
A mighty wealthy miner—
Made the biggest pile on record, boss, and
travelled 'round the earth;
He'as very grand and haughty,
And tall and dark and 40,
And the eminentest citizen in all the town of Perth.

He thought he'as Providential—
He *knew* he's influential,
Which his language it was polished and his manners up
to date:
But he'as horrid unpoliteful
If you seemed the least bit slightful,
And he'd make you feel how low you were at just 2.20 rate.

And in church he looked so mighty,
And a sorter highty-tighty,
Which his scowl was quite ferocious if you don't turn up
on time ;
And he'd freeze your very marrow—
Make you feel that you're a sparrow,
With the glare he'd cast upon you, which was terrible
sublime.

When the sermon's put in motion,
This Duke, with great devotion,
Would close his eyes and go to sleep and leave the
　　world behind ;
Pay not the least attention
When the minister did mention
That he hates to see an erring lamb a-toddling on so blind.

Then the worthy man got vicious
In a moment of capricious,
Said he'd like some better conduct from a person like
　　the Duke ;
You've seen gunpowder, maybe, boss,
When you put a match to he, boss ;
Well, those words they reached the Nabob's ear by
　　some unholy fluke.

And he got up sorter slowly,
And the worthy man and holy
Allowed he'd run his ship upon some figurative reef
When he saw him reach behind him,
And then a flash did blind him,
And the shepherd left his flock to fish, to everyone's relief.

Then the Colonel said he reckoned
That the Fates they kinder beckoned
For him to take a change of air after so loud a scene :
And he melted from the city
In a manner that was pretty ;
The church is closed and things they aint quite what
　　they might have been.

"LIKE AS A FATHER PITIETH HIS CHILDREN."

HY, O why, if pity
    Flowing from The Highest
    Could but move t'alleviate one atom of our woe,
  Why should we in sorrow
  Go through Life's long journey?
Why for other's sinfulness such trials undergo?

  Can we help that others
  Sinned before High Heaven?
Can we mortals move the Past to penitence and prayer?
  Answer! can we even
  Help ourselves—the Present?
Sinning ere we enter in this world of pain and care.

  We are shaped in evil—
  Formed in sin and trouble;
In congenial wickedness we revel all our days:
  Overpowering Evil
  Pushes us from Heaven;
Siren, dread in punishment, but pleasant to the gaze.

  See our little babies—
  Helpless mites of creatures—
Little tiger-kittens in a Cherubim's disguise;
  Amateur Beelzebubs,
  Beliels and Molochs;
Fore-ordained to live a life of evil, shame, and lies.

Pity from the Father—
Pity past the telling—
Flows unto his helpless little children here below;
Pity for our anguish,
Wickedness and blindness,
Pity for the Sin that caused our suffering and woe.

Pity that we, hapless,
Helpless and unknowing
Enter on a life we'd sever dared we be so rash:
Suffering in the body,
Anguished in the spirit,
Grovelling for the golden fruit that turns to dust and ash.

Seething world of violence,
Fury and corruption!
How thy wild, despairing cry must wring the Heart of Love;
And behold! how precious
In the sight of Heaven
Must be they whose Spirit eyes gaze on the Throne above.

Like as Stars of brightness
In a sea of blackness,
Nearly overwhelmed, yet safe by clinging to The Cross:
Suffering more than others,
Bruised, exhausted, breathless;
Striving for the Spirit Land by gentleness—not force.

Can the Great Good Spirit—
Fount of Love Undying—
Witnessing our strife with groans that words can never tell,

Can the Mighty Justice—
Forming us in weakness—
If we cannot fight the fight consign our Souls to Hell?

Look ! an earthly father
Punishes his children,
But would he to nameless woe consign them evermore ?
Would he, dying, rob them
Of their sacred birthright ?
And shall God, less merciful upon them shut the door ?

Surely we are punished
In ourselves already ;
Surely best had we remained in Nothingness Supreme :
Where that life so happy
But has tasted sorrow ?
Calmer dreamless Sleep than Sleep with e'er so blest a Dream.

But like oil on waters
Tossed full sore and troubled,
Come the words of righteous Paul, the Gentiles' mighty Saint—
Saying that the sufferings
Of this world are nothing
To the grand Hereafter that no words can ever paint.

When, the battle over,
Loosened from our bondage—
That on Earth so oft had chained our Spirits in the Past—
We shall live in Glory,
Pure throughout the ages ;
Ah ! So pure and single—free from all our pain at last.

FANCY.

WHAT would be life without thee, Spirit fair?
How very drear and barren; sunless waste!
Thou dainty Spirit, Heaven-born; when prone
Inactive lies this clay, then to the soul
Instinct thou hastest and in sweet commune
Wander through worlds unknown, and still more worlds
Unfold before thee, limitless, and each
More lovely than the last.
                    In thy soft realms
Flow brighter, purer, streams; and limpid lakes
More fair than those of earth; thy flowers more fair;
Thy birds sing songs as soothing to the ear
As may not be elsewhere, and thy sun's rays
Are ne'er eclipsed by cloud.   Thyself how fair!
I have not words to praise thee, Heavenly Sprite,
And yet, methinks, how human; but of so
Greater intensity as needs must be
In more than human stature, for methinks
Another form of thee have I at times
Beheld, and yet more forms, some sad, and some
Of fearful import, shudder-moving, stern.
Friend of my soul thou art, but, subtle Sprite
I love thee not but when thou art in mood
Calm and serene and walk'st with me in soul,
Hand clasped in hand, through the Empyrean.

Then mount we Pegasus and wing our flight
Back through the ages; for, so subtle thou,
Time melts before thee, everything to thee
Is possible and probable, thou fair
Companion of the Muses Nine, except
That thou Eternity can'st compass not.
The Never-ending, No-beginning is
To thee a Space unknown indeed, untried;
For oftentimes thy lightning plumes have fanned
The great abyss with fateful energy;
On-dashing so to win the coveted
Knowledge of what is great Eternity;
Thinking by speed to so surprise the End:
Compassing leagues of space, into that realm
Where darkness reigns and silence and the air
Is not; still on and on with vivid speed,
Hoping 'gainst hope some resting place to find;
Still on—great space, and emptiness—no End.
Now fail thy pinions, and with hasty wheel
I see thee backward wing thy baffled course
With frighted speed, for thou the wilderness
Peoplest with horrid forms, who chase thee fierce
Yet catch thee not, nor yet, indeed, could so.
'Twere pity that for human souls 'tis thus,
But thou'rt a daring and a wilful Sprite
And mischievous withal; for without thee,
In this respect, our Spirits know enough
For what they need to onward bear them through
The hosts of Satan. Come, thou god-like Sprite,

Dual parent of the Muses, conqueror
Of Time the Mighty, hoary headed sage,
And dwell with me, nor chide me that at last
The pupil greater than the master grows,
When haply for the second time in Life
The fatal voice of Great Jehovah calls
The weary Spirit from these prison-walls,
Which forth, rejoicing, leaps, and wings with speed
Its joyous flight through scenes that may have been
Familiar before, when thou it's steps
Led doubtfully, but much more bold than he ;
And so may haply look upon the face
Of God Almighty, the Eternal, Theme
Of highest contemplation, and may know
In one delicious draught all things, and bow
Adoring, satisfied.   Nor need thee more.

THE OCEAN.

OUNDLESS and glorious, wild and uproarious,
   Foam crested, bounding, rejoicing and free ;
   Crying in wanton mirth, as tho' the sober earth
      Thou would'st persuade to join revels with thee.

Melting in cloud of spray on thy resistless way,
   Tangible thou, and yet subtle as air ;
Like to a blooded horse holding his wild free course,
   Bounding with joy, free from trouble or care.

Throbbing with joyous life, raging in wanton strife,
   Laughing with glee in thy terrible power ;
Like as a tiger lies purring with half closed eyes,
   Seeming as passions could ne'er o'er thee lower.   •

Shaking thy myriad heads above thine ocean beds,
   Sighing with fulness of happy delight ;
Like little children play, out on a holiday,
   Innocent pleasures, and memories bright.

      *   *   *   *   *   *

Roaring in sullen wrath, rolling thy waters forth,
   Solemn and awesome, resistless and stern ;
Moaning in restless pain, shaking thy tawny mane,
   Sad for the past that can never return.

Hurling thy thund'rous waves on o'er drowned seamen's graves,
  Dashing in blinding spray far on the land ;
Shrieking in rage and grief, striving to find relief,
  Mad and despairing, unheeding command.

Mystic and mighty sea ! Open thine heart to me,
  Show me the secrets hid up in thy deep ;
Let my heart hear thy sighs, show me what in thee lies,
  Let me laugh with thee, and when thou weep'st, weep.

Hast thou a living soul, through centuries to roll ?
  Verily, thou to our nature art kin ;
Yes, I shall know some day all that thou can'st not say,
  Know all thy goodness and know all thy sin.

WHEN DAY IS DONE.

N the golden blaze of sunset, when the world is in
     a glow—
     A fairyland of brilliant hazy light,
I sit and watch the splendour and I think of long ago,
     While a-waiting for the coming of the night.

What a wilderness of beauty! what strange longings fill the soul;
     What great yearnings after what we cannot think;
With a wild delicious ecstacy we cannot understand:
     Sure between us and our Heaven this is the link.

When there's no one near to trouble and the world seems all alone,
     Yet the voices whisper softly to the heart;
And the songs of birds harmonious rise upward to the sky—
     Earth and Heaven do not seem so far apart.

And I see the wooded mountains with their bold majestic slopes,
     And the shadows on the trees when day is done,
With their calm reflections falling in the waters of the lake,
     In the twilight at the setting of the sun.

Comes the beauteous star of evening and the firelight flashes
     bright,
     And the sweet wild scent of woods and prairies rise;
And the birds and beasts are silent and the shadows darker grow,
     And the wondrous tints die slowly from the skies.

From the forest comes the crying of the wild cat to it's mate,
  And great moths and bats go softly flitting by,
And the night-jar screams above me with a weird and fearful call,
  And I hear afar the coyote's wild cry.

But I love these savage noises, for they speak unto my soul,
  And I love to watch the blue smoke curl and fade;
And the shadowy mountains rising to the starry sky above,
  And the firefly's torch in every woodland glade.

With the dark lake's limpid waters softly murmuring on the shore,
  Clear reflecting all the shining worlds above:
Oh, the wonder of the beauty and the life and health and joy
  In this midnight Nature's fairyland of love!

Comes soft sleep and dreamless slumber gently stealing o'er
      the soul,
  With the whispering winds to fan me into rest;
Ah, the blessedness of slumber with no canopy but sky,
  By the wild and perfumed breezes soft carressed.

Oh, those starry nights of summer! oh those nights of soft delight!
  With Nature's thousand voices far and near,
With the moonlight's bright reflection in the little dancing waves,
  Oh, my heart! what would I give to have it here!

THE GENTLE BRONCO.

 TENDERFOOT somewhere out West
Thought his riding he'd put to the test;
So he borrowed a horse
—A bucker of course,
And got down to work with a zest.

He saddled the beast in a week,
With much trouble and many a squeak,
And he chuckled "I'll show
The cowboys, you know,
What riding is like, for their cheek."

But the bronco he put up his back,
And things got considerably slack;
And the fellow went round
The moon with a bound,
And they took home the bits in a sack.

THE POET.

HERE was a fellow once and he
Thought he was some at poetry:
And so he'd sit and incubate
Ideas in his lofty pate
—Ideas that would make a poet
Go mad—'Tis well that you should know it.
He'd write about the balmy Spring,
And make up songs about the King;
Send sonnets to his lady faire
(With which she used to curl her hair),
And ravings to the lovely snow,
And other things extremely low.
He'd sit and hatch from morn till night,
His muse—poor thing—had chucked him quite:
The Editors—unlucky men—
He'd kill with doses from his pen.
Until at last one day this pill
Came on a theme that made him thrill:
'Twas *so* sublime and yet so mild,
It would not hurt a little child.
It thrilled him to his inmost core,
And as he thought he thrilled some more.
It shook him violently all day,
But what it was I cannot say;
For when next morning's sun arose,
And he had got inside his clothes,

A sudden flash of wild despair
Electrified his flowing hair:
He gasped some words to the effect
That all his great idea was wrecked;
He'd clean forgotten all the theme
Which was to fill up many a ream.
The Editors were saved—the muse
Danced a wild war-dance in his shoes.

Air—BONNIE DUNDEE.

O the West, to the West, to the land of the free,
Where the bison is mastered by Buffalo B.
And the Injine and cowboys go scooting around
With their guns in their hands and their ropes on the ground.

Come fill up my cup, come fill up my can,
Come saddle my horses and call out my men,
We'll paint the town red and then we'll ride free,
To the country of Red Shirt and Buffalo B.

THE INDIAN VILLAGE.

N the brown far-reaching prairie,
    Laden with its scented grasses,
    Lay an Indian encampment
With a little pond beside it,
Showing on its glassy surface
Clear reflection of the lodges,
Clear reflection of the Heavens,
And the waving, rustling grasses,
Yellow with the breath of summer,
Yielding wild delicious perfume
To the breeze that stole among them.
Tall the lodges, each one covered
With the skins of many bisons,
Painted with a savage grandeur—
Storied legends and traditions ;
Showing high and dreadful prowess,
Deeds of arms and mighty valour,
And the shimmering, breeze-kissed surface
Mirrored red and blue and yellow,
Mingling with the tinted grasses
And the blue of Heaven in beauty :
Coloured picture well befitting
All the coloured scene around it.
People walked among the lodges,
Clad in leather from the bison.
With a robe cast round about them
Of the skin from off the bison.

Red men—warriors tall and handsome,
Bold majestic men and valiant,
With the floating eagle feathers
Waving from the stately head dress.
Mighty chiefs with mighty records.
Slowly from the West the sunset
Tinted all the heavens with splendour,
With a gorgeous wealth of colour,
With a wealth of tinted glory.
Sank the sun into the prairie
Far away among the grasses;
Flashed upon the little lakelet
On the bosom of the prairie;
Shone upon the painted lodges;
Loth it seemed to leave the picture:
Cast the shadows far and lengthy,
Bathed them with a flood of glory,
As though ling'ring on them, sighing
" O my children, my red children,
" Not for long shall I behold thee,
" Not for long, my poor red children.
" Comes the white race from the Eastward,
" Ever flowing Westward, Westward;
" Ever, covetous and hungry,
" Casting evil eyes upon thee;
" Fare thee well, my dear red children;
" Fare thee well, my poor red children."
Down he sank, and faintly sighing
Came the chilly evening breezes,
Came the bats and came the night hawks,
Softly-flitting shapes and shadows,
Tiny voices midst the grasses
Crying softly to each other;
Shapes in air appear and vanish,
Cries go forth 'twixt earth and Heaven.

ALAS! POOR BERTIE.

E looked and felt an aristocrat,
    With patent boots and a smart top hat,
    He wasn't too thin and he wasn't too fat,
  But just the proper size.
Which his name was Bertie and also Jinks,
And he'as awfully proud of himself, methinks,
For I saw him giving satisfied winks
  With one of his other eyes.

And oh! the ladies who passed him by,
With parasols and a business eye,
And very small feet and a heap of dye,
And hair which I think they could hardly deny
  Was sold by the " bang " or " switch."
And they glanced with approval upon the " toff "
Whose father had taken the Malakoff
(So he said) and had one of his limbs shot off,
  But couldn't remember which.

And a gay old dowager duchess bold,
Who must have been quite 29 years old,—
Though 20 was what she always told—
And who had been left 50 years in the cold,
  Came strolling along one day ;
And switched off the youth like a bud in spring
Is switched from the bough by the bug on the wing,
And gathered away to a lingering
  Death.   That's the end of this lay.

THE WARNING.

HAT is this sound from the desert? this sound as of
wailing and woe?
To-night is my spirit disturbed by a voice from the
past long ago.
What is this voice that disturbs me? what is the message it
brings?
Borne on the North Wind I hear it, but what are the words
that it sings?

To-night is the desert uneasy, the vultures retire not to rest,
But sail in great circles afar o'er the prairies, away, far away to
the West :
And the long colored grasses are crying—a wierd, whisp'ring
cry of affright ;
What shall befall us, great Sun, when thou goest and cometh
the night?

The buffalo run in their myriads, the white-headed eagles sail
high ;
A voice is among them that whispers "Beware ye, for danger
is nigh !"
And the wind sweeps along o'er the prairies and cries with a
strange warning sound :
What is this that I know not the words of, that is known to all
nature around?

Dark clouds are afar on the prairies, the face of Manitto is hid;
He sees not the woes of his children, he remembers the deeds
that they did !

Yet will we not bow to your nation as others before us have
     bowed,

We will fight and Manitto will love us and smile upon us from
     the cloud.

How can a danger come nigh us? We are men and our hearts
     know not fear,

And our lances' sharp points are our answers.   I have spoken.
     The answer is here.

Soft words are for women: we heed not.   We will fight you,
     nor make any truce

From the chivalry of the Apaches to the far away tribes of the
     Sioux.

And, bethink'st thou, the " Queen of the Prairies "* shall e'er
     bow her neck to the foe?

We are warriors born.   Then beware thou.   Let my brother
     consider, and go!

Are our warriors women? Go, ask them! Our vengeance we'll
     show to thee soon,

If thou'lt come with the braves of Navajo and ride in the
     " Mexican Moon." †

We will carry the war to your thresholds and sweep o'er the
     land like a flood ;

Our war-clubs will answer entreaties ; our lances be drunken
     with blood.

---

* The Comanches.
† The annual foray into Mexico: on one occasion as far South as
Durango.

We will drive you afar from our country; in your land shall be
mourning and woe,
When thou meetest our warriors in battle—the raiders of far
Durango.

Count the scalps on my warriors' leggings ! See, the blood on
the knife : It is yours !
My young men have smitten the war post ! We will fight to the
last for our cause.
Wilt thou dare stand before us in battle ? 'Tis good ! we will
give back your blows,
And will drag at the tails of our mustangs the last of the race
of our foes.

The post is set up for the torture, the splinters are waiting the fire,
The knives of my brothers are ready—they await but the
coming Messiah.
Our lances are keen for the slaughter ; the eagles are screaming
on high ;
The Moon-of-the-Leaves is approaching. In my ears I can hear
the war-cry.

   *   *   *   *   *   *

In my dreams I have seen a dark vision : an eagle came down
from the sky
And took away all of our warriors far up to the Prairies on high :
Where hunger and cold may not enter, nor white men may
trouble our state.
But what means this vision ? I know not. The mystery of
it is great.

"LONE WOLF,"* DIED 1892.

CHILD of the prairies of the West,
  Could'st thou have known
   Thou ne'er would'st see thy native land again,
The wild free plains whereon thou once did'st roam,
The sunset glories and thy warrior's home,
Would'st thou have grieved?

A stranger, dying in a stranger's land,
Laid in the soil of these thy conquerors,
Coming from thy land to the land of those
Who wrought thy race's fall.

An Indian Chief, a warrior with a name;
Wreaker of vengeance dire on foemen brave;
When in the Happy Hunting Grounds thy name is called
Wilt thou be there?

My brother's heart is strong; tears are for women;
The trail is dark but foemen smooth the way
Up to the Spirit Land and lead the war-horse forward
To bear thee to the everlasting plains.

---

* "Lone Wolf" was buried at Brompton Cemetery. He was the only
Indian who ever led a successful attack on a fortified position, and " his
body was a mass of saber and bullet wounds " got in his many wars.—B.M.

Few, few are left
Of all thy warrior brethren;
Manitto calls thee, let my brother go:
Nor grieve thy body lies not with thy fathers
In thy far home.

The fight is o'er,
The long, long dreary years of earth
Are past for thee:
The Everlasting Plains before thee lie:
Thy mustang's feet are on the narrow pathway
That leads to Heaven.

THE RAILWAY MEN.

RUSH for the train—
 The whole crowd insane
 Which the cars wont contain—
 And the porters remain
To tuck in the ends of the crowd;
  And cram 'em in,
   ram 'em in,
   jam 'em in,
   slam 'em in,
While they lift up a voice somewhat loud:—
  "O, right away, there!
  "Just you hump it, you sir!
"Now will you git in and don't lose yer back hair."
  Then the baggage they collar,
  With wild whoop and hollar,
And language most shocking (perhaps) to a "skollar."
  And jump it in,
   bump it in,
   thump it in,
   clump it in,
   plump it in,
   hump it in,
   dump it in,
   scrump it in,—
Things hum, you can bet your last dollar.

  *   *   *   *

When it's time to get out,
There's a terrible rout,
Things go flying about,
And each railway lout
Pounces down like a bad case of blizzard:
And the sleepers they wake 'em up,
   snake 'em up,
  shake 'em up;
  scare 'em out,
 flare 'em out,
tear 'em out,
stare 'em out;
 smack 'em out,
  whack 'em out,
   hack 'em out,
    back 'em out;
   pick 'em out,
  lick 'em out,
  stick 'em out,
 kick 'em out;
And the language that's used—!
And the way you're abused——!!
If you weren't so cross you'd be very amused.
And the luggage they bring it out,
    fling it out,
   sling it out;
   slash it out,
   crash it out,
  bash it out,
  dash it out;
  hash it out,
  clash it out,
 smash it out,
 flash it out;
And you dwindle away, feeling sadly ill-used,
And having all hints of assistance refused.

COMPANIONS IN SIN.

HE bloody fight was over, the corsair's devilish crew
Swarmed o'er the captured merchantman and ran-
sacked her all through.

And the sun sank down in red and gold into the opal waves,
Where so many murdered mariners were hurled into their graves.
Not scatheless had the pirates come from out the horrid fray,
For more than one upon the deck had bled his life away
With a horror and a darkness as his guilty soul stepped forth
Red-handed and profane to meet the awful God of Wrath.
And one there lay with an ashy face and a bullet through his
lung,
And the words he strove to utter forth expired upon his tongue.
A young, slight form—so young to die! and die in such a cause!
With the awful doom the pirate dared when he went against
Heaven's laws.
And his dark eyes closed and his brow was wet with the icy
drops of Death,
And the blood came forth in a thin red stream with each quick
drawn, gasping breath ;
And the rings of gold in his ears gleamed bright in the setting
sunlight ray,
And his long black hair lay all spread abroad as his life-blood
ebbed away.
Upon his breast his hands were clasped, as though he would
pray—to whom?
And a bitter smile played o'er his lips as he thought of his
certain doom.

And then he cast his hands apart, upturnéd as in mute appeal;
O, for an hour of precious life, to pray for his future weal!
Pray for his future weal? Ah, no! he'd played-and lost-the game;
And he would not show the white flag now-he'd live and die the same
Beside him knelt a comrade, a stern, hard featured man,
With his face convulsed with silent grief, and black with smoke
    and tan.
And his hands were clasped in agony as he looked on his
    comrade's form,
Together they'd gone through deeds of blood and weathered
    many a storm.
And the youth was dear as a son to him, and as on his knees he fell
He prayed—perchance the first for years—that they might
    meet—in Hell.
The end was near approaching—the white face grew more white,
The shuddering eyelids opened wide once more upon the light.
And a horror gathered in his eyes and deadly fright and fear,
And they grew more dark with terror as the end approached
    more near.
"My boy! my boy!" his comrade cried, "would I might die for thee!
"But ah, how can I dare to face the doom that thou dost see?
"Yet I must die, and die alone, nor 'chance may meet thee, dear,
"A fearless life I've led till now, and why *now* should I fear?
"I come with thee, my boy; and see, I take thee by the hand,
"We'll live together, as in life so in the other land."
A flash of steel—a spurt of blood—a shivering gasping cry—
As down upon the deck he sank, so both of them did die.
And thus they went : just two dead men 'midst several other dead:
And hand in hand the souls went forth, and both their hands
    were red.

ARMS AND A HERO.

HERE was once a mighty warrior well versed in
ancient lore,
   And "many snows" had o'er him passed, though
much less than a score;
But in old tradition's doings he was equal to the best,
And used to try and make himself a most obnoxious pest.

He'd read about the Wyandottes, the Pawnees and Choctaws,
The Seminoles and Rapahos, Cheyennes and Omahaws;
The Modocs and the Utes were as brothers to his mind,
And he guessed he'd leave the Mohicans in valour far behind.

He loved the Delawares, for was not Uncas of that race?
And Chingachgook the warrior who fought at Chevy Chase?
But the Wichitas and Blackfeet, the Foxes, Kaws and Creeks,
In his imagination were a beastly set of sneaks.

He called himself "The-man-who-scorns-to-look-you-in-the-face,"
And used to wear a blanket and a horrible grimace;
And the tribe that he belonged to was undoubtedly the Sioux,
By the utter lack of common sense he used to introduce.

He tried to scalp the tabby with a knife which he had "raised,"
But retired from out the conflict with a nose most badly grazed;
And the plumed affair upon his head went badly to the deuce,
And the wampum belt was ruined and the war-paint got quite
loose.

But undeterred this warrior would leak about the house,
And try to emulate the noble savage and the mouse;
As if he thought an "Injun brave" did nothing but get tight,
And imitate a crocodile from morning until night.

He'd grunt with vim and energy and say that he "had spoke,"
And look annoyed if you just tried to take it for a joke;
Which he wore a shield of painted skin slung kinder on his back,
But his dress was unathletic and uncomfortably slack.

The blanket used to trip him up when on a noiseless trail,
And the shield in falling caused most expeditions to fail;
And 'twas wounding to the dignity of such a warrior bold,
To be found a-crawling down the stairs, and consequently sold.

And 'twas one too many for that child when one sad dreadful
    night
He got locked out from hearth and home, alone and in a fright:
His frantic war-whoop failed to reach "the-great-white-father's"
    ears,
Nor could he find the big brass bell and most got drowned
    in tears.

And so he gave the war-path up and laid his weapons down,
Buried the axe, returned the robe and washed off all the brown:
And as for many a by-gone raid he still expected blame,
A "citizen of eminence" he right away became.

FAIRYLAND.

OW oft, how oft in dreamland, comes a sweet voice to me,
Over the mirroring waters, over the tropic sea;
Where the breezes are heavy with perfume and the
skies so blue and deep,
And the songs of birds fall soft on the ear, in my beauteous
land of sleep.

Where the yellow sands roll onward, kissed by the golden sun,
And the wavelets' rippling music soothes to rest when day is done;
And the depths of sky are wondrous blue and the waving sea
below
Is clear to the beds where the little shells seem wavering to
and fro.

And ah! for the marvellous tints and shades and the wealth of
colour there,
Where the seaweed spreads its rarest forms, and flows like
mermaid's hair;
And the sunlight streams through the fairy glades and flashes
from burnished scales,
Where the fish dart through in their merry play and where
Nautila sails.

And ah! for the plunge through those liquid depths, 'midst the
gardens of the sea,
Where to live is life untrammeled, from every trouble free.
Where is that land of happiness, can such a region be?
In the dreamland of sleep and contentment it is given to you
and to me.

"Those liquid depths."

THE WESTERN STATES OF AMERICA.

AND of the setting sun, home of the free,
  Cradle of heroes bold,
  Storehouse of yellow gold;
  O while I sing, unfold
Thy spell o'er me,
   Fill me with the spirit of the West.

Where are thy firstborn sons, red warriors bold?
  Fighting the white man's trains,
  And lust of golden gains?
  Ask of thy woods and plains
Where 'neath the mould
   Their forgotten bodies are at rest.

Where are those names of old, fresh to my mind?
  Kit Carson, Daniel Boone?
  All gone; alas, too soon:
  Gone to their final doom,
Leaving behind
   Names among the bravest and the best.

Warriors of Western fame, gone on that trail
  Leading to Heaven's gate,
  Where their old comrades wait;
  Custer, the last, his fate
Met without quail,
   Leaving like a man at God's behest.

Rise in thy might and strength, freedom and health,
  Type of the land's first state,
  Let not thy charms abate;
  O'er lands less loved of Fate
Pour forth thy wealth,
   Soothe them with thy balm and give them rest.

ROMANCIA IN ABSURDÃ.

HERE was a girl 19 years old,
  Whose manner was extremely bold :
  'Tis true she lived in Idaho,
Which sometimes makes a maiden so.
She'd ride a horse just like a man,
And do most things a fellow can ;
And fetch the ace at 20 yards,
And swindle anyone at cards,
Take whiskey straight and throw a rope,
And ne'er had heard of Brooks's soap.
She wore long boots and Greaser spurs,
To satisfy a whim of hers,
Smoked cigarettes and said "you bet,"
And was as fast as you could get.

One day she met a band of Sioux,
And finding 'twas no earthly use
For *1* to try and flee when *10*
Were in pursuit, and they all men,
She checked her mustang's headlong speed,
And 'gan to roll herself a "weed."
"Now don't be bashful, boys," she cried,
"Sorry to give you such a ride,"
And at the chief she winked aloud,
Which rather took that worthy crowd.

They carried her away, of course,
And made themselves with grinning hoarse ;
And hinting that the " Pale-faced squaw "
Was very much " All thar "—and more.
And what a caution she would be
If " Itching-palm "—their chieftain—he
Saw fit to marry her—Great Scott !
They 'gan to get a nervous lot,
And rather wished they hadn't spied
That little maid with hat-brim wide.

Now " Itching-palm " thought just the same,
And felt that he was much to blame
In taking to his tribe this squaw—
His feelings hurt him more and more :
And she was whistling out in glee
" Maud, come into the grounds with me ; "
And winked at any reckless brave
If e'er a look at her he gave.
The warriors quite frightened got—
One thought pervaded all the lot—
That she their chieftainess would be
And give them beans enough for three.
She'as sure to be revengful, too,
And visit this unlucky *coup*
With tenfold vengeance on their head—
Each son of Uncas wished he'as dead.
Their chieftain, too, the worthy man,
Got scared as any chieftain can.

The problem that he lit on was
Uncommon difficult, because
He saw no earthly answer would
Do him or his tribe any good.
The thought of *marrying* that girl
Made even *his* straight hair to curl.
But that was what he caught her for—
He'd rather welter in his gore !
And then he dared not make her wed
With " Dirty-face "—his heir, and head
Of nearly half of all his tribe,
For he allowed that as a bribe
To that same chief to let her be
A ruling power as well as he
She'd cut *his* throat and just raise Cain—
The thought it caused him fearful pain.
He knew not what on earth to do,
It turned his tint from red to blue.

Meanwhile the pace at which they " got "
Began to lessen quite a lot ;
In great uncertainty they rode,
And awful hesitancy showed.
The girl she noticed this, and said,
" Cheer up, my bully warriors red ;
" You look as if you'd seen a ghost—
" You are a pretty slender host.
" I guess you'd mosey at a bound
" If I began to climb around.

" Come, cheer up, boys, and come along,
" And I'll give you another song."
And to their horror she began
To sing "Oh, I'm a good young man."
And she rode in the front of all,
And after her the lot did crawl ;
Not daring, when she told them " Come,"
To turn the other way and hum.

At last she said she guessed they'd camp,
And all of them with spirits damp
Assented, no one *dared* say no,
But O, How They All Wished SHE'D GO.
One thought he'd put the matter straight,
But then allowed he'd better wait.
And so they squatted for the night,
But couldn't eat, they're in such fright.
One son of Uncas took a sack
To gather wood—and came not back :
And still one more forgot that he
Was due in camp on time for tea.
The girl she sang and ate like mad,
And poor old " Itching-palm " looked bad.
He wished that *he* could gather wood,
But as a chief of course he could
Not do such thing, despite his plight,
Nor take to ignominious flight
Like any of the baser crew,
Who don't care what on earth they do.

But he'as in horrible alarm
For fear of being alone with " Marm;"
And vowed he take no captives more
If he lived up to seven score.

His warriors one by one vamosed,
Although at last this was opposed;
As the survivors thought if they
Were caught alone they'ld have to pay
A fearful vengeance for the rest;
And this black thought their souls opprest.
Then Madam said, " Well, boys, I've heard
" Your conduct's more or less absurd—
" Especially more—but let that pass;
" Your boss, there, seems a special ass;
" But how you all can sit and be
" So silent just lays over *me*,
" And don't you please forget it, boys—
" For goodness' sake don't make a noise."
So gently chaffing them she kept
Till every warrior nearly wept.
" To-morrow, boys," continued she,
" You'll all come back along with me;
" And straight to Uncle Sam you'll go
" For treating of a lady so.
" It's bed-time now, so say ' good-night.'
" And either go to sleep or fight."
Her words struck terror to their hearts—
They made a note to " 'Ware of Tarts."

And each one meekly tried to go
To sleep, but failed in doing so.
But Madam, trusting to their fright
To keep them safe, slept through the night.

Now, when each warrior saw that she
Was sound asleep—or seemed to be,
The crowd arose as though one man,
And then an eager time began.
But " Itching-palm "—although his name
Was working over all the same,
Turned him with his sustaining pride
Toward his sleeping, almost bride,
Bowed reverently and raised his eyes
Up to the starry midnight skies.
He thought—he dared not speak outright,
Standing alone with her that night—
" Keep her, Great Spirit, through this life—
" This girl, who *nearly* was my wife :
" For verily, this maiden is
" Great in capacity for biz ;
" And has demoralized my men,
" Although she's 1 and we were 10.
" Yet whisper soft that ' Itching-palm '
" Held unto her no thought of harm.
" Thus ' Itching-palm ' doth to thee pray "—
She moved—the chief moved, too—away.
And when next morning Madam rose,
And stretched herself and blew her nose,

She found the camp deserted quite,
And couldn't help but laugh outright.
" Those poor old Johnnies, now," quoth she,
" Fancy at them believing me."
And so she had a lonely meal,
But finished with a Highland Reel ;
For when she went to get her horse,
Thinking to find him gone, of course,
She found one—truly not her own—
But one whose sinew, shape and bone
Proved him to her admiring eyes
A veritable equine prize.
And fastened to the saddle-horn
A note—" From one whose heart you've torn."
'Twas all.   The thing was very clear—
Something so far and yet so near.
And one had left for her that steed—
To bear her back again with speed.
And as she thus their feelings learned
She slowly murmured, " Well I'm derned !"

A FEW OPINIONS OF THE PRESS
ON THE FIRST EDITION.

"*Saturday Review*," 25th *April*, 1891.

The style and humour of Mr. Metchim's "Wild West Poems" (Fisher Unwin) so far beggar description as to cry aloud for illustration. Here is a stanza that is fairly representative of the poet's manner:—

I guess when I was strolling down
    The centre of the street,
A boss Tornado boomed along
And grupped me by the feet.

"*Morning Post*," 7th *April*, 1891.

Mr. T. Fisher Unwin publishes a collection of "Wild West Poems," composed and illustrated by B. Metchim. They are all intensely American, and some of them are full of quaint and amusing conceits. There is no lack of spirit and fun in either the verses or the illustrations, and those who enjoy American humour will find plenty to amuse them in "Wild West Poems."

"*Daily Chronicle*," 13th *May*, 1891.

To judge from the contents, the volume of "Wild West Poems" (London: Fisher Unwin) is appropriately named. These "poems," for the most part, are like nothing produced in any other quarter of the globe. They are mainly written in the dialect peculiar to the Wild West; and they embody the requisite kind of incidents and actors. One of the collection, "Sam Blackburn's Ride," is told with considerable power; others must be called clever. The author writes occasionally in a serious vein, not without skill. There are some apt illustrations.

"*Lloyds'*," 28th *March*, 1891.

There is a certain class of American poetry which has a wild flavour about it that is quite refreshing to poor Britishers, unaccustomed to the everyday use of the revolver and the tomahawk. Mr. B. Metchim is the composer and illustrator of a little volume of "Wild West Poems" of this kind, published by Mr. Fisher Unwin, and bearing on the cover an appropriate Wild West "figure-head" that speaks for itself. The verse, in various metres, is diverting, chiefly by its truly native slang. It must be confessed, however, that in some of the lines only an American could possibly discover the rhyme. The illustrations are most eccentric.

"*News of the World*," 12th *April*, 1891.

Commended: B. Metchim's quaint "Wild West Poems." (T. Fisher Unwin, &c.)

"*Scotsman*," 30th *March*, 1891.

A shilling volume of "Wild West Poems," composed and illustrated by Mr. B. Metchim, has been published by Mr. T. Fisher Unwin, London. They are chiefly ballads of adventure with more incident than poetic merit in them. They give some amusing examples of Western slang and Western manners and customs in belligerency. The book is one rather for the dialect reciter than for the lover of poetry.

"*Glasgow Herald*," 26th *March*, 1891.

"Wild West Poems," composed and illustrated by B. Metchim, and published by Mr. T. Fisher Unwin, is a shilling volume of rhymed yarns about b'ars and Injuns, and snakes and stage-drivers, and the other stock property of the American humorist. Some of the tales are exceedingly "tall."